LEVEL 6 Supplemental

EXAM SERIES

By Glory St. Germain ARCT RMT MYCC UMTC &
Shelagh McKibbon-U'Ren RMT UMTC

ULTIMATE
MUSIC THEORY

GSG MUSIC

Enriching Lives Through Music Education

ISBN: 978-1-990358-13-5

The Ultimate Music Theory™ Program

Enriching Lives Through Music Education

The Ultimate Music Theory™ Workbooks & Answer Books Program includes:

UMT Rudiments Workbooks for Prep 1, Prep 2, Basic, Intermediate, Advanced & Complete
UMT Exam Series (Set #1 & Set #2) for Preparatory, Basic, Intermediate & Advanced

Supplemental Workbooks for PREP LEVEL, LEVELS 1 - 8 & COMPLETE LEVEL
UMT Supplemental Exam Series for LEVEL 5, LEVEL 6, LEVEL 7 & LEVEL 8

The Ultimate Music Theory Program is the *Way to Score Success* as UMT helps students prepare for nationally recognized theory examinations including the Royal Conservatory of Music.

Library and Archives Canada Cataloguing in Publication. UMT Workbooks & Exam Series /Glory St. Germain & Shelagh McKibbon-U'Ren. Respect Copyright. All rights reserved. GlorylandPublishing.com

Ultimate Music Theory Rudiments Exam Series

GP - EPS1	ISBN: 978-1-927641-00-2	Preparatory Rudiments Exams Set #1
GP - EPS1A	ISBN: 978-1-927641-08-8	Preparatory Exams Answers Set #1
GP - EPS2	ISBN: 978-1-927641-01-9	Preparatory Rudiments Exams Set #2
GP - EPS2A	ISBN: 978-1-927641-09-5	Preparatory Exams Answers Set #2
GP - EBS1	ISBN: 978-1-927641-02-6	Basic Rudiments Exams Set #1
GP - EBS1A	ISBN: 978-1-927641-10-1	Basic Exams Answers Set #1
GP - EBS2	ISBN: 978-1-927641-03-3	Basic Rudiments Exams Set #2
GP - EBS2A	ISBN: 978-1-927641-11-8	Basic Exams Answers Set #2
GP - EIS1	ISBN: 978-1-927641-04-0	Intermediate Rudiments Exams Set #1
GP - EIS1A	ISBN: 978-1-927641-12-5	Intermediate Exams Answers Set #1
GP - EIS2	ISBN: 978-1-927641-05-7	Intermediate Rudiments Exams Set #2
GP - EIS2A	ISBN: 978-1-927641-13-2	Intermediate Exams Answers Set #2
GP - EAS1	ISBN: 978-1-927641-06-4	Advanced Rudiments Exams Set #1
GP - EAS1A	ISBN: 978-1-927641-14-9	Advanced Exams Answers Set #1
GP - EAS2	ISBN: 978-1-927641-07-1	Advanced Rudiments Exams Set #2
GP - EAS2A	ISBN: 978-1-927641-15-6	Advanced Exams Answers Set #2

Ultimate Music Theory Supplemental Exam Series

GP-L5E	ISBN: 978-1-990358-11-1	LEVEL 5 Exams
GP-L5EA	ISBN: 978-1-990358-12-8	LEVEL 5 Exams Answers
GP-L6E	ISBN: 978-1-990358-13-5	LEVEL 6 Exams
GP-L6EA	ISBN: 978-1-990358-14-2	LEVEL 6 Exams Answers
GP-L7E	ISBN: 978-1-990358-15-9	LEVEL 7 Exams
GP-L7EA	ISBN: 978-1-990358-16-6	LEVEL 7 Exams Answers
GP-L8E	ISBN: 978-1-990358-17-3	LEVEL 8 Exams
GP-L8EA	ISBN: 978-1-990358-18-0	LEVEL 8 Exams Answers

Go to UltimateMusicTheory.com **and check out the FREE Resources**

Ultimate Music Theory FREE RESOURCES created just for you!

Ultimate Music Theory
LEVEL 6 Supplemental Exams

Table of Contents

Score: **60 - 69** Pass; **70 - 79** Honors; **80 - 89** First Class Honors; **90 - 100** First Class Honors with Distinction

Ultimate Music Theory: *The Way to Score Success!*

The 2016 RCM Theory Syllabus **additional concepts** to the Level 6 (formerly Intermediate Rudiments) Examination Requirements covered in the **UMT Supplemental LEVEL 6 Workbook** include:

♫ **Rhythm and Meter**: Dotted sixteenth notes and rests.

♫ **Scales**: Parallel Major and minor keys.

♫ **Chords and Harmony**: Dominant 7th Chords in Root Position, in close or open position. Identification of Authentic (V-I or V-i) Cadences and Half (I-V; IV-V or i-V; iv-V) Cadences on a Grand Staff using root position triads in Major and minor keys, in Keyboard Style. Application of Functional Chord Symbols (I, i, IV, iv, V, V7) and Root/Quality Chord Symbols (for example, C, Am, G7) for the implied harmonies of a melody using root position chords.

♫ **Melody and Composition**: Composition of a Question-Answer Phrase pair (antecedent - consequent) in a Major key, given the first two measures to create a Parallel Period.

♫ **Form and Analysis**: Identification of concepts from this and previous levels (in the 2016 Theory Syllabus) within short musical examples.

♫ **Musical Terms and Signs**: New Terms and Signs have been added.

♫ **Music History**: Introduction to Musical Styles of the Baroque and Classical Eras: Invention in C Major, BWV 772 (J.S. Bach); Brandenburg Concerto No. 5, BWV 1050 (J.S. Bach) and Eine Kleine Nachtmusik (W.A. Mozart).

Study and Memorize the UMT Map - LEVEL 6

Circle of Fifths

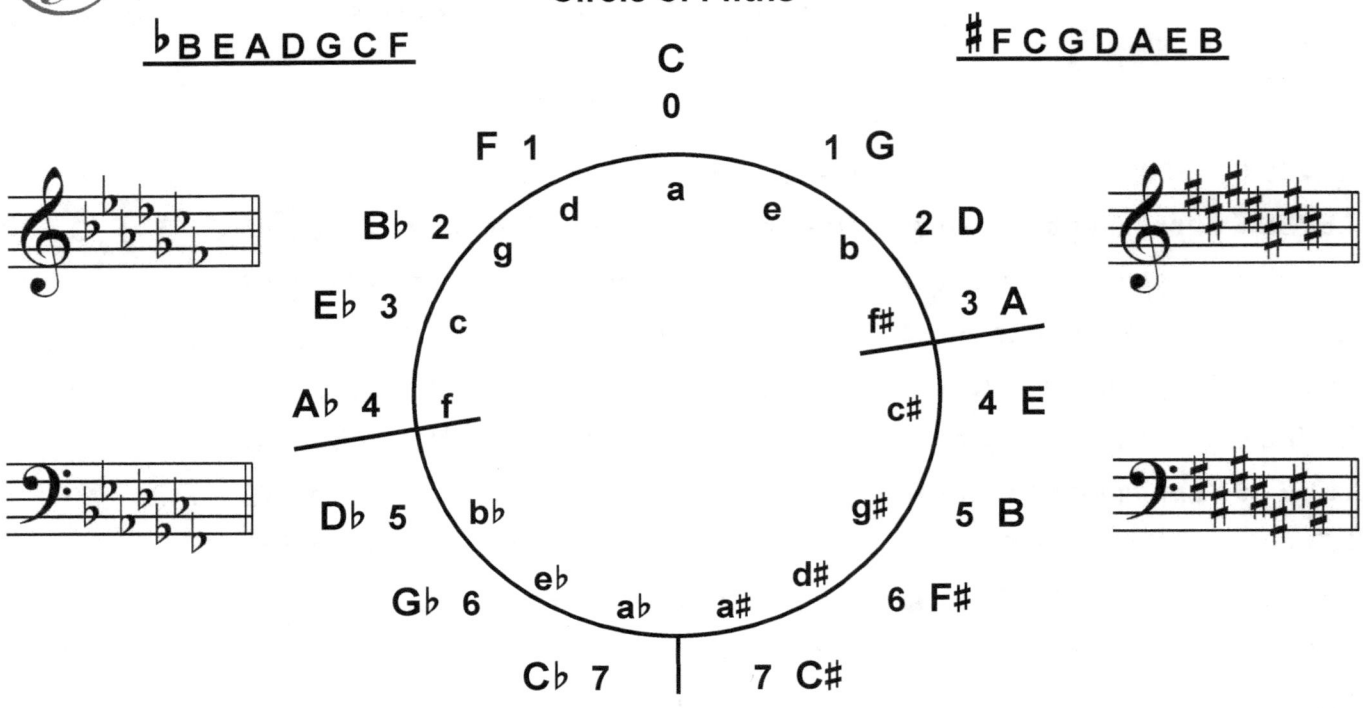

♭B E A D G C F

♯F C G D A E B

C 0
F 1   1 G
B♭ 2   2 D
E♭ 3   3 A
A♭ 4   4 E
D♭ 5   5 B
G♭ 6   6 F♯
C♭ 7   7 C♯

d a e b
g c f#
c bb c#
f bb g#
eb ab a# d#

20th Century Scales

Notes	
9	Octatonic scale
7	Whole Tone scale
7	Blues scale (↑4th or ↓5th)
6	Pentatonic scale:

Major - no 4th and 7th degrees

minor - no 2nd and 6th degrees

Scale Degree   Technical Name

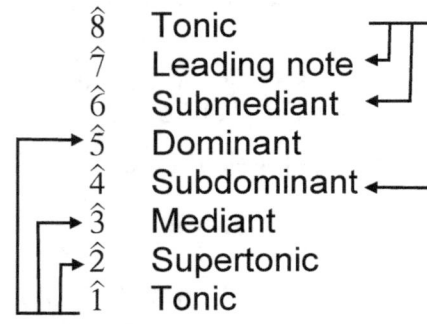

$\hat{8}$ Tonic
$\hat{7}$ Leading note
$\hat{6}$ Submediant
$\hat{5}$ Dominant
$\hat{4}$ Subdominant
$\hat{3}$ Mediant
$\hat{2}$ Supertonic
$\hat{1}$ Tonic

Subtonic - Degree $\hat{7}$ of Natural Minor Scale

Cadences

	Major	minor
Authentic: (Perfect)	V - I	V - i
Half: (Imperfect)	I - V or IV - V*	i - V or iv - V*

(*no common note, voices descend)

Melody Writing

Parallel Period: a + a1

Contrary Period: a + b

Intervals   ## Accidentals

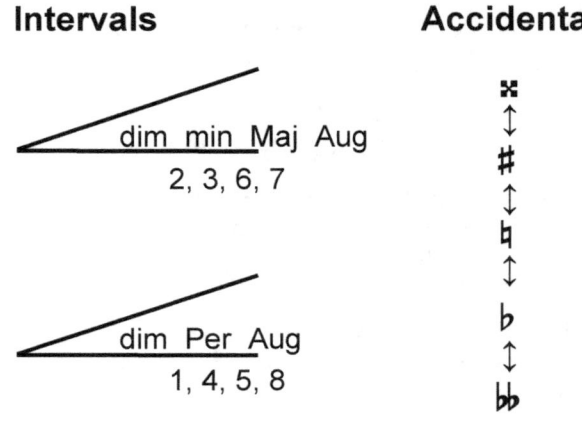

dim min Maj Aug
2, 3, 6, 7

dim Per Aug
1, 4, 5, 8

Exam Tip: Copy the UMT Map for LEVEL 6 below. Using a blank piece of paper, write out the UMT Map from memory before beginning each practice exam and the final exam.

Circle of Fifths

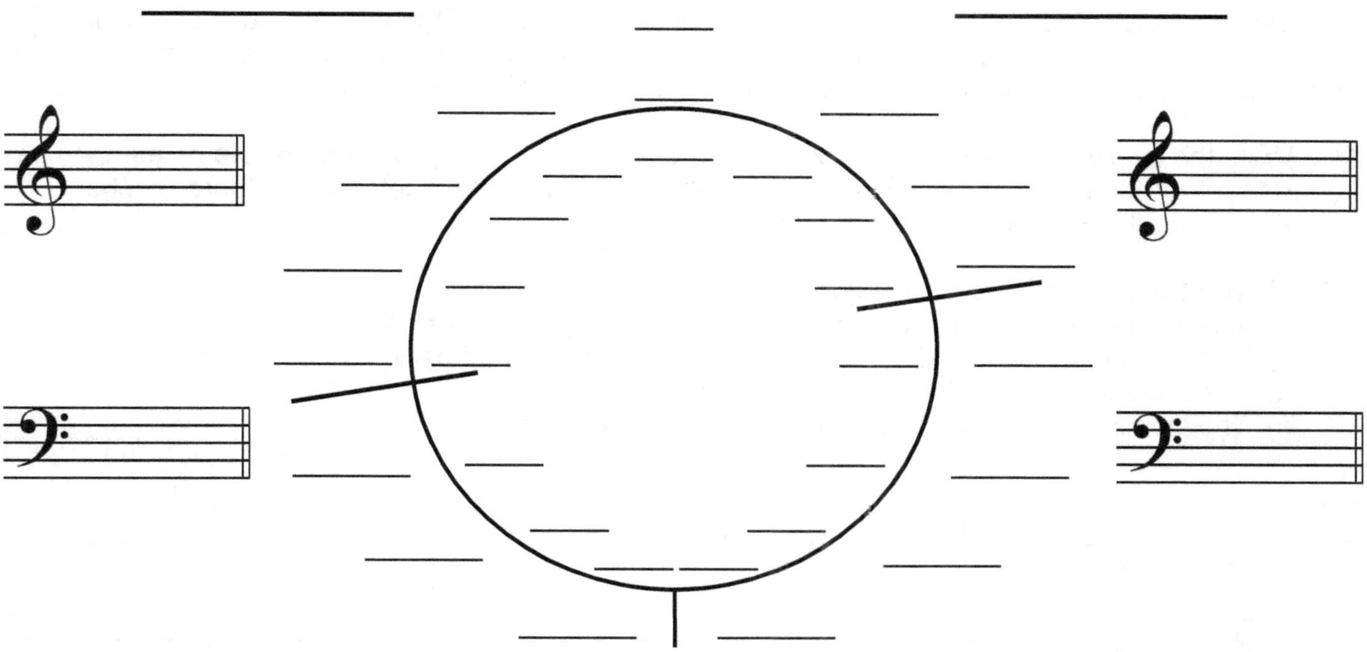

_____   ___   _____

Notes   **20ᵗʰ Century Scales**

___ _____ scale

___ _____ scale

___ _____ scale (↑___ or ↓___)

___ _____ scale:

_____ - no ___ and ___degrees

_____ - no ___ and ___degrees

Cadences   Major   minor

_____: ____ - ____   ____ - ____
(Perfect)

_____: ____ - ____   ____ - ____
(Imperfect)   or   or
            ____ - ____*   ____ - ____*

(*no _____ note, voices _____)

Melody Writing _____ Period: a + ___

_____ Period: a + ___

Scale Degree   Technical Name

___ _____
___ _____
___ _____
___ _____
___ _____
___ _____
___ _____

_____ - Degree ___ of Natural Minor Scale

Intervals   **Accidentals**

___ , ___ , ___ ,

___ , ___ , ___ ,

Ultimate Music Theory
LEVEL 6 Supplemental Exam #1

Total Score: ____
50

Use with Intermediate Exam Set #1 - Exam #1

The Ultimate Music Theory™ Intermediate Rudiments Workbook, LEVELS 5 & 6 Supplemental Workbooks, Intermediate Rudiments Exam Series and LEVEL 6 Supplemental Exams prepare students for successful completion of the Royal Conservatory of Music Level 6 Theory Examination.

1. Write the following Close Position Solid (Blocked) Triads and Chords. Use whole notes. Use a Key Signature and any necessary accidentals. Write the Root/Quality Chord Symbol above and the Functional Chord Symbol below.

10   a) The Supertonic Triad of D Major, in first inversion.
    b) The Submediant Triad of d minor harmonic, in second inversion.
    c) The Dominant Seventh Chord of b minor harmonic, in root position.
    d) The Mediant Triad of E Major, in second inversion.
    e) The Dominant Seventh Chord of A flat Major, in root position.

Root/Quality
Chord Symbol: a) _____   b) _____   c) _____   d) _____   e) _____

Functional
Chord Symbol: a) _____   b) _____   c) _____   d) _____   e) _____

2. For each of the following Open Position Triads and Chords, write the Root/Quality Chord Symbol above each Triad and Chord.

10
Root/Quality
Chord Symbol: a) _____   b) _____   c) _____   d) _____   e) _____

3.   For the following Melodic Opening:

       a) Name the key of the melody.
       b) Write the Time Signature directly on the music.
___
10   c) Complete the first phrase according to the given Functional Chord Symbols. End on an
          unstable scale degree. (There will be more than one correct answer.)
       d) Compose an Answer Phrase to create a Parallel period. End on a stable scale degree.
          (There will be more than one correct answer.)
       e) Draw a phrase mark (slur) over each phrase.

Key: _____

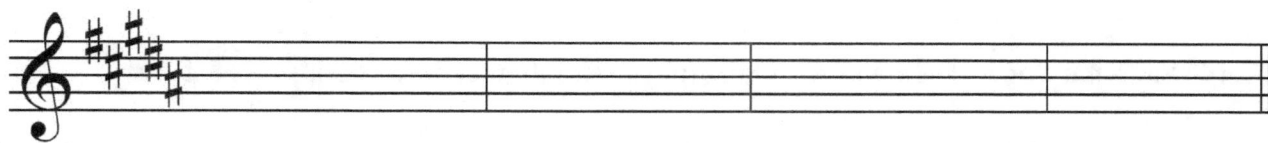

4.   For each of the following Melodic Phrases:

       a) Name the key of the melody.
       b) Write the Time Signature directly on the music.
___
10   c) Write the Root/Quality Chord Symbols implied by the melody on the lines above the music.

Root/Quality
Chord Symbol:

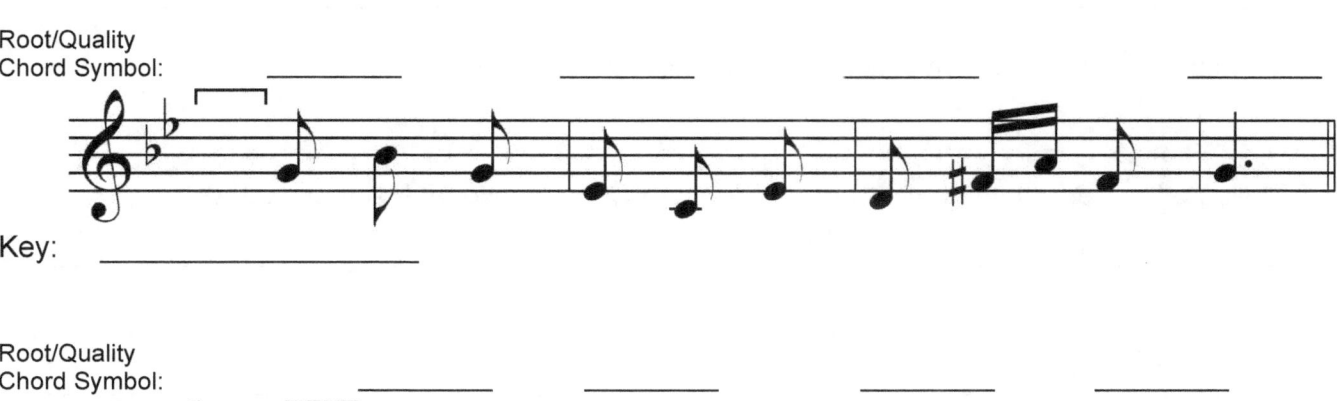

Key: _____

Root/Quality
Chord Symbol:

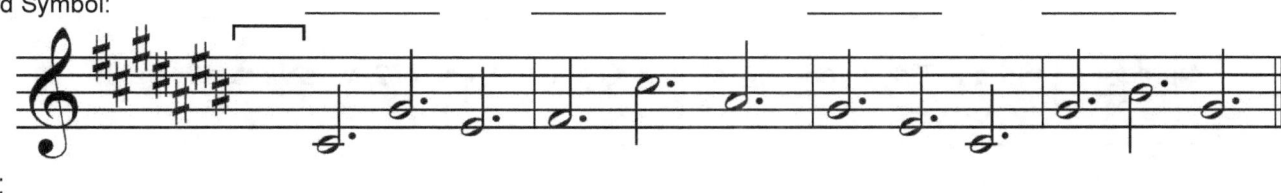

Key: _____

5. Answer any 10 (Ten) of the following questions.

    a) Name the Composer of "Invention in C Major, BWV 772".

10 _____

    b) Name the Composer of "Eine kleine Nachtmusik, K 525, first movement".

    _____

    c) Name the Genre of "Eine kleine Nachtmusik, K 525, first movement".

    _____

    d) Name the Genre of "Brandenburg Concerto No. 5, first movement".

    _____

    e) Name the Structure of "Brandenburg Concerto No. 5, first movement".

    _____

    f) Name the Form of "Eine kleine Nachtmusik, K 525, first movement".

    _____

    g) Name the Performing Forces of "Eine kleine Nachtmusik, K 525, first movement".

    _____

    h) Name the Performing Forces of "Invention in C Major, BWV 772".

    _____

    i) Name the Texture of "Invention in C Major, BWV 772".

    _____

    j) Name the Performing Forces of "Brandenburg Concerto No. 5, first movement".

    _____

    k) Name the key of "Eine kleine Nachtmusik, K 525, first movement".

    _____

    l) Name the Period or Era when "Invention in C Major, BWV 772" was written.

    _____

1.   For each of the following phrases:

a) Name the key of the phrase.
___ b) Write the Time Signature directly on the music.
10 c) At the Cadence, write the Root/Quality Chord above and the Functional Chord Symbol below.
d) Name the Type of Cadence (Authentic or Half).

Root/Quality
Chord Symbol: _____ _____

Functional
Chord Symbol: _____ _____

Key: _____   Cadence: _____

Root/Quality
Chord Symbol: _____ _____

Functional
Chord Symbol: _____ _____

Key: _____   Cadence: _____

2. a) Name the following intervals.

_____ _____ _____ _____ _____

b) Change the upper note of each interval enharmonically. Rename each interval.

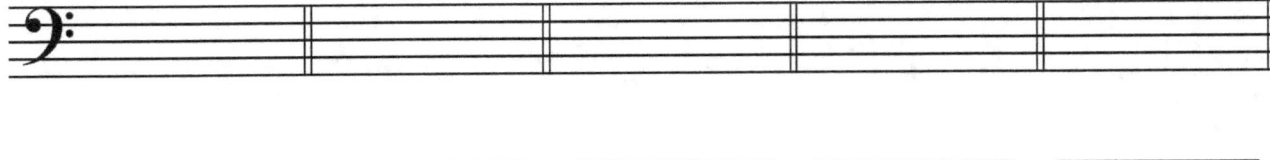

_____ _____ _____ _____ _____

3. Identify the Root, Quality (Major, minor or Dominant 7th) and Position of each Chord or Triad.

Root: _____ _____ _____ _____ _____

Quality: _____ _____ _____ _____ _____

Position: _____ _____ _____ _____ _____

Root: _____ _____ _____ _____ _____

Quality: _____ _____ _____ _____ _____

Position: _____ _____ _____ _____ _____

4.   Write the definition for each of the following signs.

a) 𝄟.   _____

$\overline{10}$ b) ▬   _____

c) *8va*   _____

d) ⌢   _____

e) ∨   _____

f) ❜   _____

g) ⚏   _____

h) 𝄋   _____

i) 𝄴   _____

j) 𝄵   _____

5.   Match each musical term or sign with the English definition. (Not all definitions will be used.)

Term		Definition
tranquillo	c	a) too much
subito	_____	b) less
troppo	_____	~~c)~~ quiet, tranquil
grave	_____	d) smooth
meno	_____	e) animated, lively
quasi	_____	f) left hand
non	_____	g) return to the normal register
animato	_____	h) as if, almost
legato	_____	i) suddenly
loco	_____	j) slow and solemn
senza	_____	k) not
		l) without

$\overline{10}$

Ultimate Music Theory
LEVEL 6 Supplemental Exam #3

Total Score: _____
       50

Use with Intermediate Exam Set #1 - Exam #3

1. For the following Melodic Opening:

    a) Name the key of the melody.
    b) Write the Time Signature directly on the music.
    c) Complete the first phrase according to the given Functional Chord Symbols. End on an unstable scale degree. (There will be more than one correct answer.)

    _10_

    d) Compose an Answer Phrase to create a Parallel period. End on a stable scale degree. (There will be more than one correct answer.)
    e) Draw a phrase mark (slur) over each phrase.

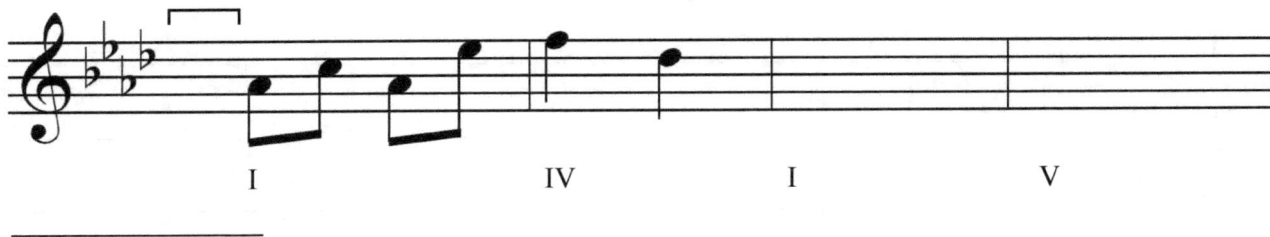

Key: _____

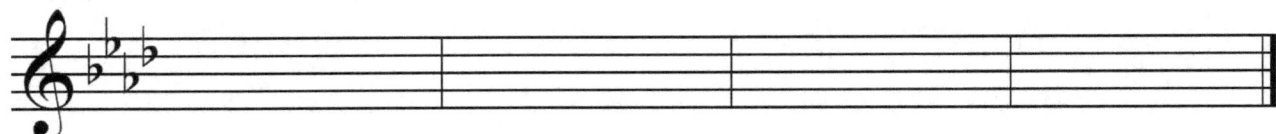

2. Write the following Close Position Solid (Blocked) Triads and Chords. Use whole notes.
    Use a Key Signature and any necessary accidentals. Write the Root/Quality Chord Symbol above and the Functional Chord Symbol below.

    _10_

    a) The Submediant Triad of g sharp minor harmonic, in first inversion.
    b) The Dominant Seventh Chord of A Major, in root position.
    c) The Subdominant Triad of f minor harmonic, in second inversion.
    d) The Supertonic Triad of G Major, in first inversion.
    e) The Mediant Triad of D flat Major, in second inversion.

Root/Quality
Chord Symbol: a) _____   b) _____   c) _____   d) _____   e) _____

Functional
Chord Symbol: a) _____   b) _____   c) _____   d) _____   e) _____

3.   a) Write a broken (ascending) Major triad in root position above each of the following notes.

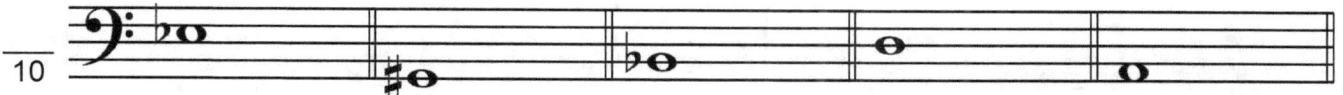

10

   b) Write a broken (ascending) minor triad in root position above each of the following notes.

4.   Write the term or word that each of the following statements applies to. Use the following terms or words. (Not all terms and words will be used.)

   Concerto Grosso   Imitation   Homophonic   Chamber Music   Invention

10   Polyphonic   Sequence   Baroque   Motive   Exposition   Ritornello Form

   a) _____ - The immediate repetition of a motive in a different part or voice (same or different pitch).

   b) _____ - Two or more consecutive repetitions of a motive in the same part or voice at a higher or lower pitch.

   c) _____ - A texture with a single line of melody that is supported by a harmonic or chordal accompaniment.

   d) _____ - The first section of sonata form that states the main themes (usually 2 contrasting themes).

   e) _____ - A short melodic or rhythmic fragment that is used to build a melody.

   f) _____ - A genre of music for a small ensemble with one player per part.

   g) _____ - A keyboard composition in polyphonic texture that is based on imitation.

   h) _____ - A Baroque orchestral work, usually in three movements, performed by a Concertino and Ripieno.

   i) _____ - A texture that is a combination of two or more independent melodic lines, also called counterpoint.

   j) _____ - A form often used in the first and third movements of a Concerto Grosso.

5. Analyze this excerpt from Johann Philipp Kirnberger's Les carillons by answering the questions below.

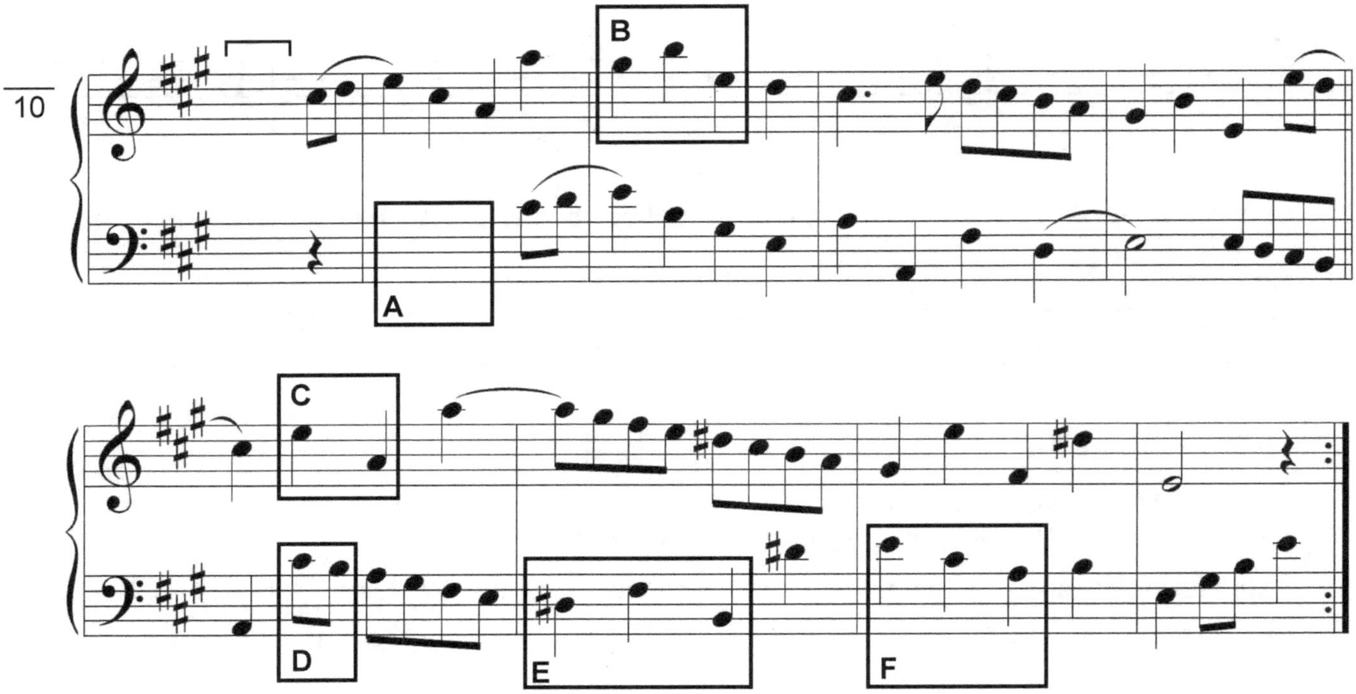

a) This piece is in Cut Time. Add the correct Time Signature directly on the music.

b) At **A**, add the missing rest(s). Identify the rest(s) used: _____.

c) For the triad at **B**, identify: Root: _____;   Quality: _____;   Position: _____.

d) Circle an example of the triad (melodic & rhythmic pattern) at **B**, written one octave lower.

e) Identify the interval at **C**: _____. Identify the interval at **D**: _____.

f) For the triad at **E**, identify: Root: _____;   Quality: _____;   Position: _____.

g) For the triad at **F**, identify: Root: _____;   Quality: _____;   Position: _____.

h) In this excerpt, identify the number of: Slurs: _____;   Ties: _____.

i) Explain the bar line at the end of the excerpt? _____.

j) When this excerpt is performed, how many measures are played? _____.

Total Score: ____
50

1.　a) Following the Root/Quality Chord Symbols, write each Solid (Blocked) Triad or Chord.
　　　Use whole notes. Use accidentals.

Root/Quality
Chord Symbol:　　Em　　　　　A♭7　　　　　G♯m/B　　　　B♭/F　　　　A♯m

　　b) Write the Root/Quality Chord Symbol above each Triad or Chord.

Root/Quality
Chord Symbol: _____　　_____　　_____　　_____　　_____

2.　For each of the following Melodic Phrases:

　　a) Name the key of the melody.
　　b) Write the Time Signature directly on the music.
　　c) Write the Root/Quality Chord Symbols implied by the melody on the lines above the music.
　　d) Name the type of cadence (Authentic or Half) implied by the melody.

10

Root/Quality
Chord Symbol:　　　_____　　　　　　_____　　　　　_____

Key: _____　　　　　Cadence: _____

Root/Quality
Chord Symbol:　　　_____　　　　　　_____

Key: _____　　　　　Cadence: _____

3. For each of the following Cadences:
    a) Name the key.
    b) Name the type of cadence (Authentic or Half).

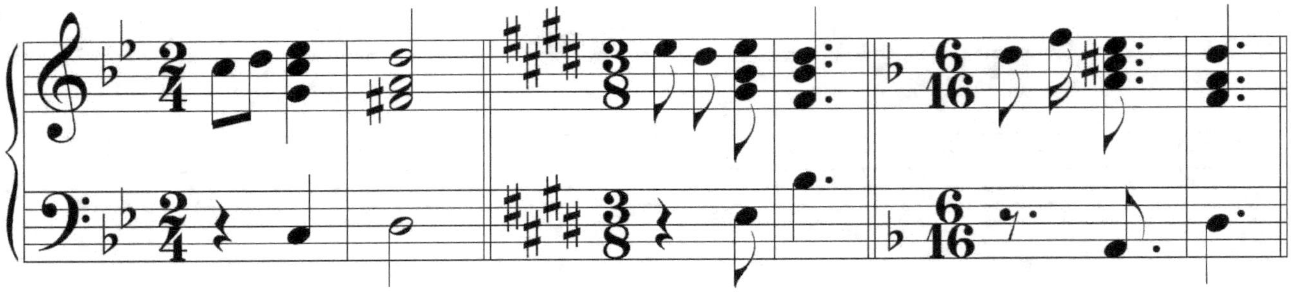

Key: _____   _____   _____

Cadence: _____   _____   _____

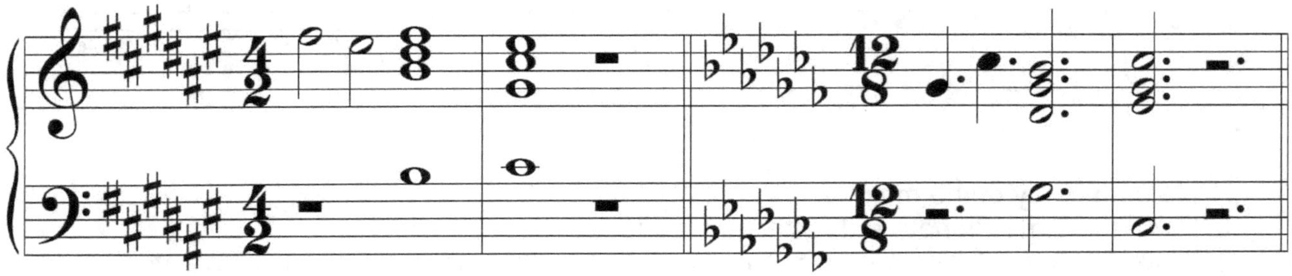

Key: _____   _____

Cadence: _____   _____

4. Name the key (Major or minor) for each of the following Dominant Seventh Chords.

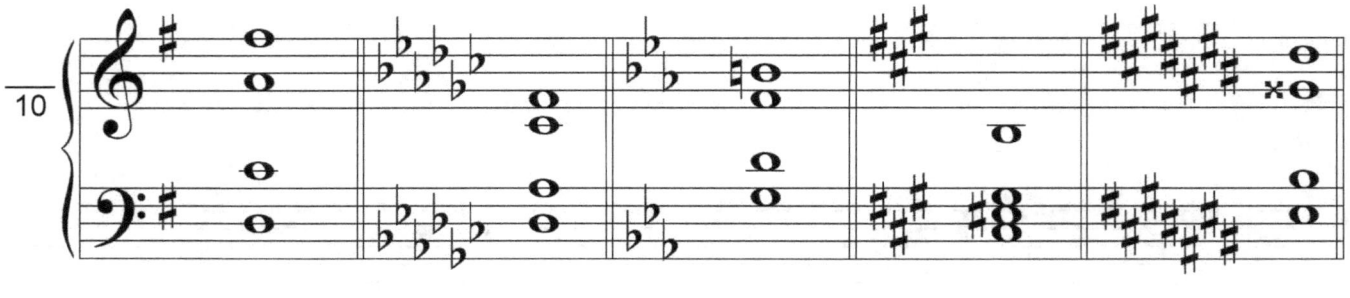

Key: a) _____   b) _____   c) _____   d) _____   e) _____

5.   Analyze this excerpt from Clementi's Sonatina in C Major Opus 36, Number 3, Movement III by answering the questions below.

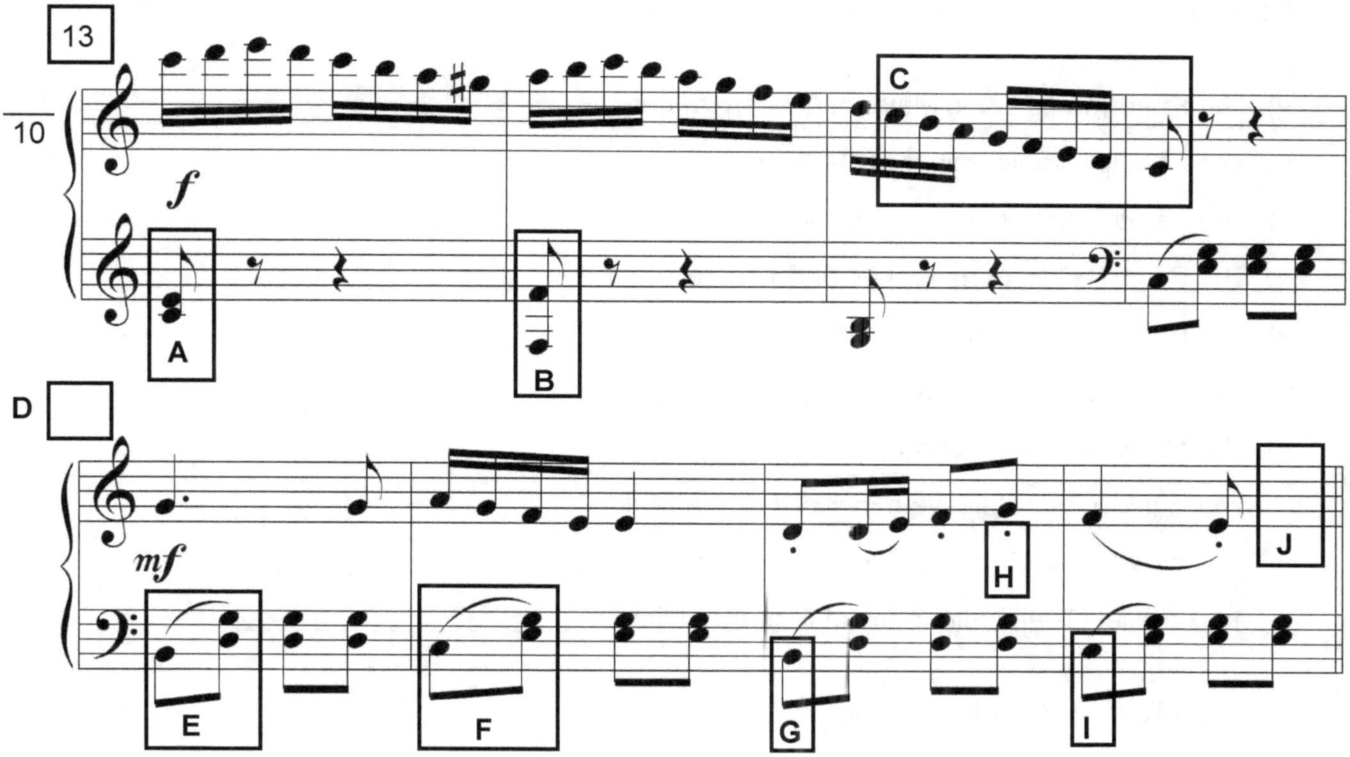

a) For the Interval at **A**, name the notes: _____ _____.   Name the interval: _____.

b) For the Interval at **B**, name the notes: _____ _____.   Name the interval: _____.

c) Name the scale at **C**.   _____.

d) This excerpt begins on Measure 13. Add the correct Measure Number at **D**.

e) For the triad at **E**, identify: Root: _____;   Quality: _____;   Position: _____.

f) For the triad at **F**, identify: Root: _____;   Quality: _____;   Position: _____.

g) Identify the Technical Degree Name of the note at **G**.   _____.

h) Explain the articulation sign at **H**.   _____.

i) Identify the Technical Degree Name of the note at **I**.   _____.

j) Add the missing rest at **J**. Name the type of rest used.   _____.

1. Name the Major or minor key for each of the following.

___ a) The Enharmonic Tonic Major of C sharp Major. _____

10 b) The Parallel (Tonic) minor of D Major. _____

c) The Relative minor key of C flat Major. _____

d) The Parallel (Tonic) minor key of B flat Major. _____

e) The Enharmonic Tonic minor of b flat minor. _____

f) The minor key with 6 flats. _____

g) The Major key with 7 sharps. _____

h) The Enharmonic Relative minor of F sharp Major. _____

i) The Enharmonic Relative Major of b flat minor. _____

j) The Parallel (Tonic) minor key of F sharp Major. _____

2. For the following Melodic Opening:

a) Name the key of the melody.
___ b) Write the Time Signature directly on the music.
10 c) Complete the first phrase according to the given Functional Chord Symbols. End on an unstable scale degree. (There will be more than one correct answer.)
d) Compose an Answer Phrase to create a Parallel period. End on a stable scale degree. (There will be more than one correct answer.)
e) Draw a phrase mark (slur) over each phrase.

Key: _____   I   IV   I   V

3. a) Write the Root/Quality Chord Symbol above each Triad or Chord.
    b) Rewrite each Chord or Triad in Close Root Position in the Single Treble Staff below.

Root/Quality
Chord Symbol: _____ _____ _____ _____ _____

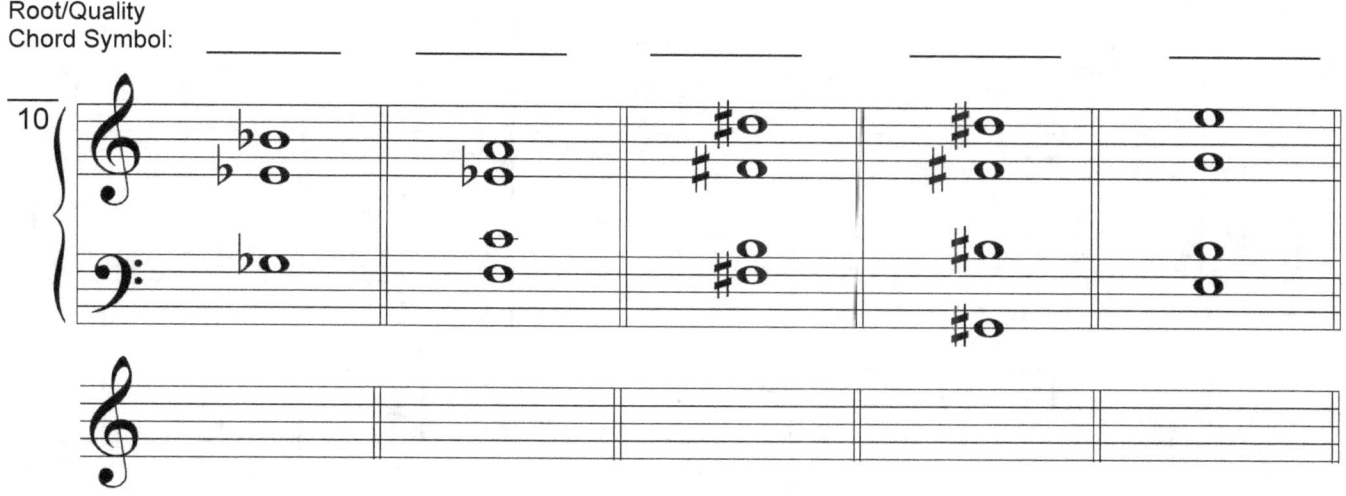

4. Circle TRUE or FALSE for each of the following statements.

a) TRUE   or   FALSE   - Wolfgang Amadeus Mozart was a Composer in the Classical Era.

b) TRUE   or   FALSE   - J.S. Bach was a Composer in the Baroque Era.

c) TRUE   or   FALSE   - "Eine kleine Nachtmusik" is written for solo keyboard.

d) TRUE   or   FALSE   - "Brandenburg Concerto No 5" features a trumpet solo.

e) TRUE   or   FALSE   - "Invention in C Major" features sequences and inversions.

f) TRUE   or   FALSE   - The first movement of "Eine kleine Nachtmusik" is in Sonata form.

g) TRUE   or   FALSE   - The predominant texture of Bach's "Invention" is monophonic.

h) TRUE   or   FALSE   - The Ritornello in "Brandenburg Concerto No. 5" begins in D Major.

i) TRUE   or   FALSE   - "Invention in C Major" is a 4-part Invention in Choral/SATB Form.

j) TRUE   or   FALSE   - The opening theme of "Eine kleine Nacthmusik" is known as the "Rocket Theme".

5. Analyze this excerpt from Jean Théodore Latour's Sonatina in G Major, Movement III by answering the questions below.

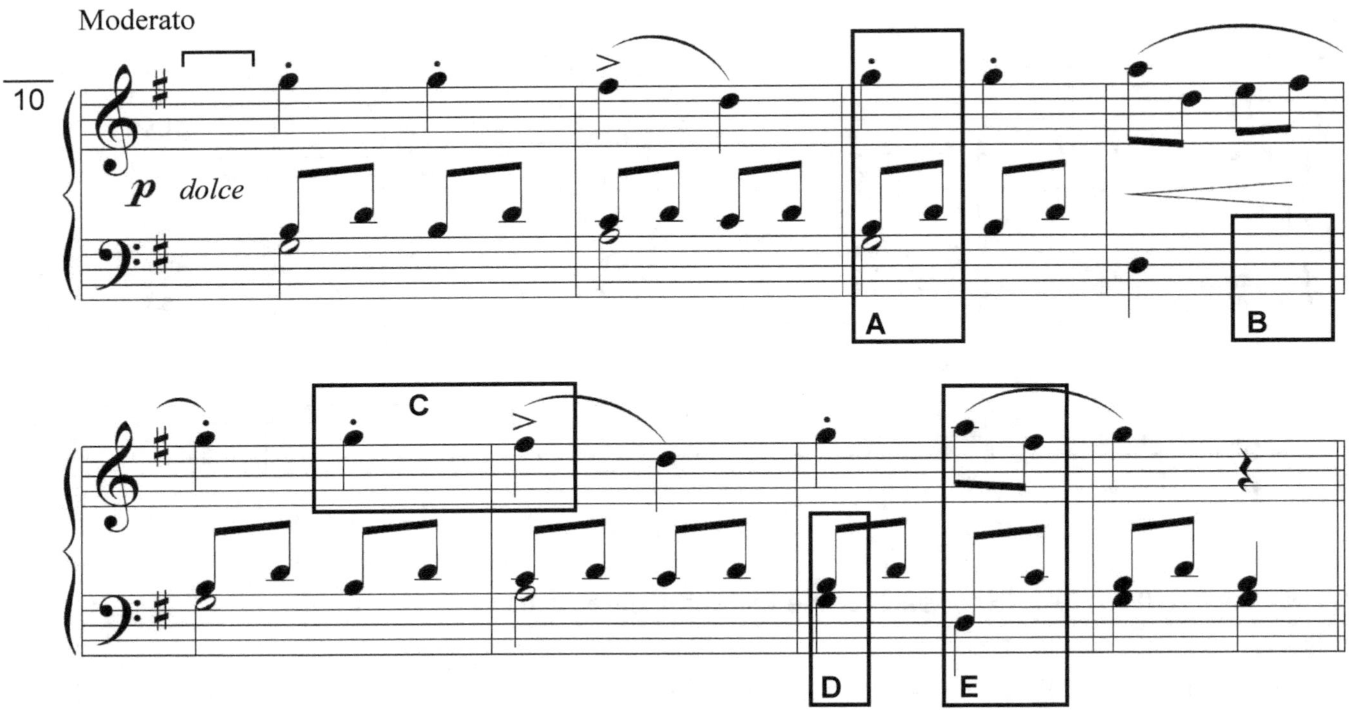

Moderato

p *dolce*

a) Name the Key. _____ Identify the Key Signature. _____

b) Add the Time Signature directly on the excerpt.

c) Explain the meaning of: Moderato: _____ *dolce*: _____.

d) Circle if the relationship between mm. 1 - 4 and mm. 5 - 8 is: a and a1   or   a and b.

e) For the chord at **A**, identify: Root: _____;   Quality: _____;   Position: _____.

f) Add the missing rest at **B**. Name the type of rest used.   _____.

g) For the Interval at **C**, name the notes: _____ _____.   Name the interval: _____.

h) For the Interval at **D**, name the notes: _____ _____.   Name the interval: _____.

i) For the chord at **E**, identify: Root: _____;   Quality: _____;   Position: _____.

j) Identify the number of: Slurs: _____;   Staccatos: _____;   Accents: _____.

1. Write the following Chords and Triads in Close Position. Use whole notes. Observe the Key Signature and use any accidentals as necessary.

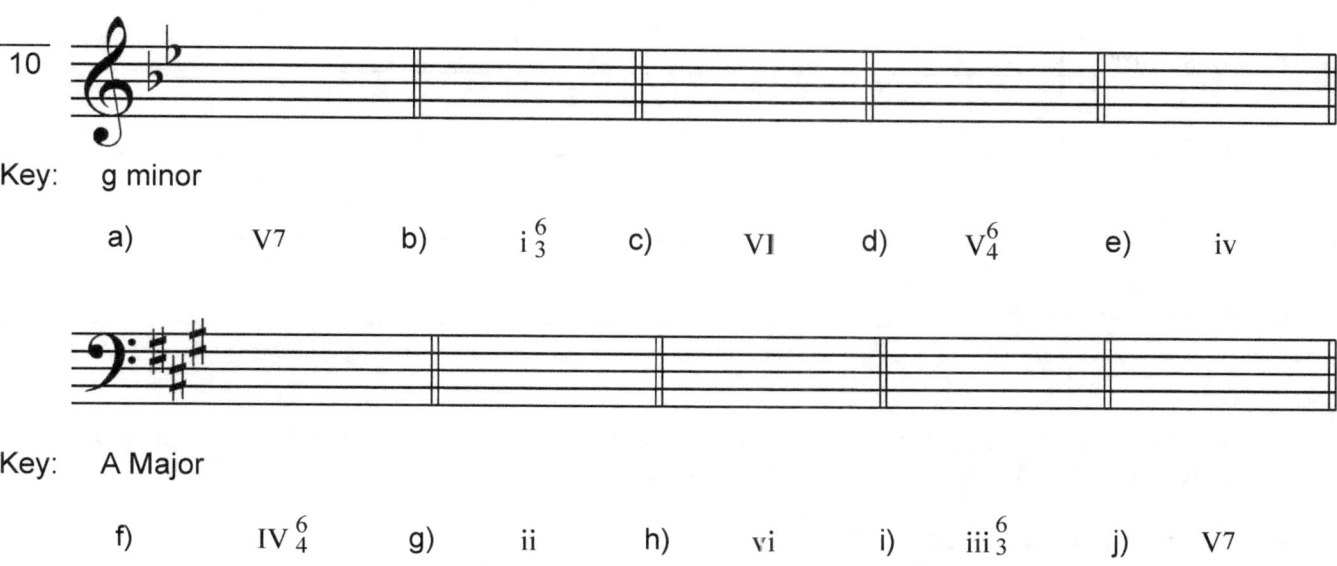

10

Key: g minor

a) V7   b) i_3^6 c) VI   d) V_4^6 e) iv

Key: A Major

f) IV_4^6 g) ii   h) vi   i) iii_3^6 j) V7

2. For the following Melodic Opening:

   a) Name the key of the melody.
   b) Write the Time Signature directly on the music.

10 c) Complete the first phrase. End on an unstable scale degree. (There will be more than one correct answer.)
   d) Compose an Answer Phrase to create a Parallel period. End on a stable scale degree. (There will be more than one correct answer.)
   e) Draw a phrase mark (slur) over each phrase.

Key: _____

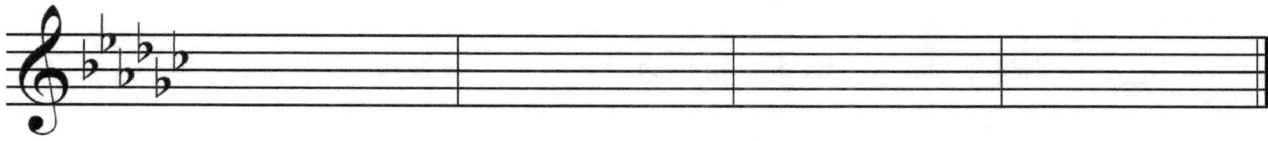

3. Explain the meaning of the following terms.

    a) *tre corde*: _____.

 ___
 10 b) *ad libitum*: _____.

    c) *senza pedale*: _____.

    d) *con fuoco ed animato*: _____.

    e) *forte e ben marcato*: _____.

4. Identify the work to which each of the following statements applies by writing the appropriate letter (A, B or C) in the space before each statement.

    A - Invention in C Major, BWV 772
 ___ B - Brandenburg Concerto No. 5, BWV 1050, first movement
 10 C - Eine kleine Nacthmusik, first movement

    a) _____ This work is part of a set of 6 Concerti Grossi.

    b) _____ This work was composed by W.A. Mozart.

    c) _____ This work opens and closes in Ritornello Form.

    d) _____ The Genre of this work is Chamber Music.

    e) _____ This work opens with a disjunct Theme 1 known as the "Rocket Theme".

    f) _____ The predominant texture of this solo keyboard work is Polyphonic Texture.

    g) _____ This work features Motives, Countermotives, Sequences, Inversions & Augmentation.

    h) _____ The Concertino in this work features the harpsichord (or cembalo), violin & flute.

    i) _____ The Ripieno in this work features a full string orchestra.

    j) _____ The form of this work is Sonata Form.

5. Analyze this excerpt from Cornelius Gurlitt's Sonatina in a minor Opus 214, No. 4, Movement III by answering the questions below.

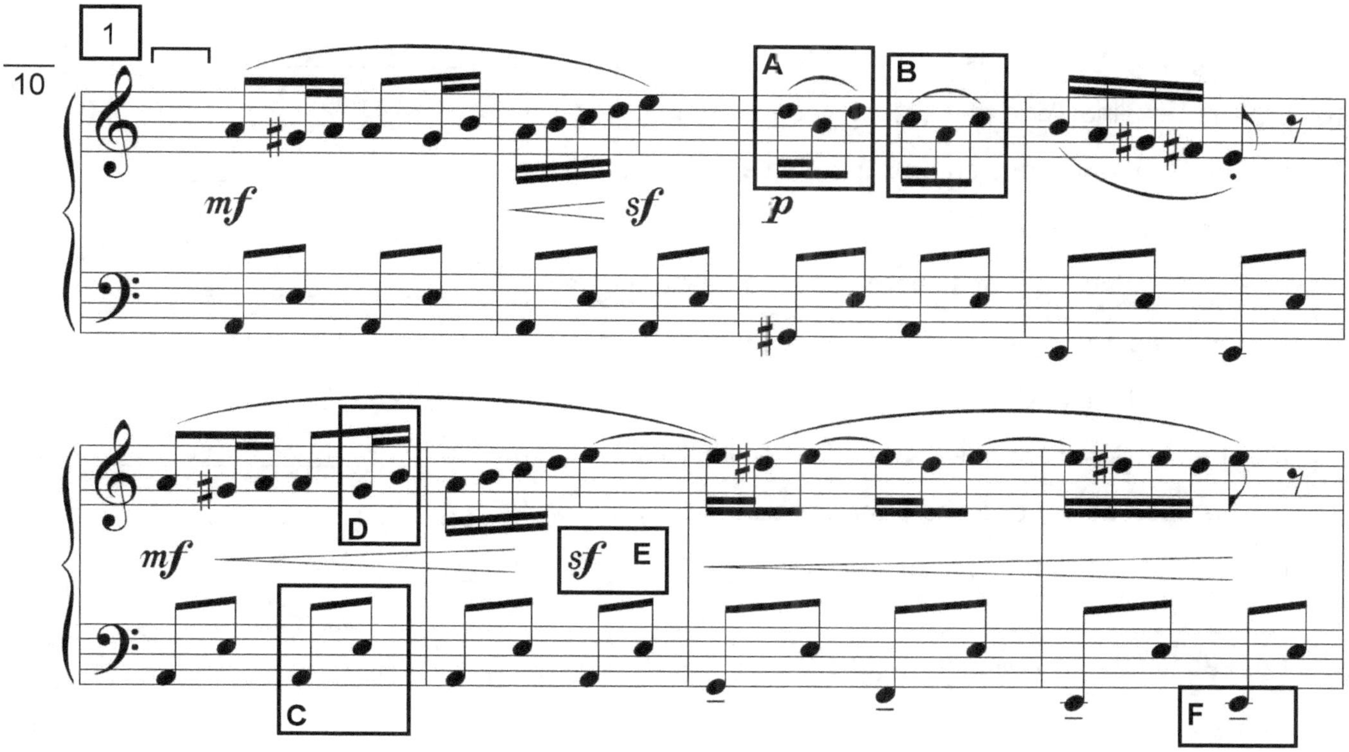

a) Name the key of this excerpt. _____.

b) Write the Time Signature directly on the music.

c) Circle to identify the movement of the notes in the Bass Clef as: Conjunct   or   Disjunct.

d) Circle the relationship of the melodic pattern at **A** and **B** as: Transposition   or   Inversion.

e) Explain the accidentals in Measure 4. _____.

f) For the Interval at **C**, name the notes: _____ _____.   Name the interval: _____.

g) For the Interval at **D**, name the notes: _____ _____.   Name the interval: _____.

h) Explain the sign at **E**. _____.

i) Explain the sign at **F**. _____.

j) Identify the number of: Slurs: _____;   Ties: _____;   Crescendos: _____.

Ultimate Music Theory
LEVEL 6 Supplemental Exam #7

Total Score: _____
50

Use with Intermediate Exam Set 2 - Exam #3

1. Name the notes (letter names) for the following Technical Degrees:

    a) The Subtonic of d minor scale, natural form. _____

 __10__ b) The Leading Tone of e flat minor scale, harmonic form. _____

    c) The Supertonic of c sharp minor scale, harmonic form. _____

    d) The Submediant of F sharp Major scale. _____

    e) The Subdominant of d sharp minor scale, harmonic form. _____

    f) The Leading Tone of C flat Major scale. _____

    g) The Mediant of D flat Major scale. _____

    h) The Subdominant of a sharp minor scale, harmonic form. _____

    i) The Submediant of g sharp minor scale, harmonic form. _____

    j) The Dominant of A flat Major scale. _____

2. For each of the following musical excerpts:

    a) Name the key.
    b) Use the notes from the melody to write one triad in Root Position on the single staff below
        each example. Use whole notes.
 __10__ c) Identify the Root, Quality and Position of each Triad.

    i) Measure 1 from "Burlesca",   ii) Measure 37 from "Prelude BWV 999",
        by Johann Ludwig Krebs   by Johann Sebastian Bach

    Key: _____   Key: _____

    Root: _____   Root: _____

    Quality: _____   Quality: _____

    Position: _____   Position: _____

3. Provide an answer (the term or the sign) for each of the following.

 a) A dynamic sign that means "loud, then suddenly soft": _____

 __10__ b) A term that means "suddenly": _____

 c) A sign that means "take a breath and/or slight lift": _____

 d) A term that means "more movement, quicker": _____

 e) A term that means "less movement, slower": _____

 f) A term that means "the upper part of a duet": _____

 g) A term that means "the lower part of a duet": _____

 h) An articulation sign that means "a stressed note": _____

 i) A term that means "with some freedom of tempo to enhance musical expression": _____

 j) A dynamic sign that means "a sudden strong accent of a single note or chord": _____

4. Write the following Triads or Chords. Use a Key Signature and any necessary accidentals. Use whole notes.

 a) The Submediant Triad of F sharp Major, in second inversion.

 __10__ b) The Subdominant Triad of e flat minor harmonic form, in root position.

 c) The Dominant Seventh Chord of e minor harmonic form, in root position.

 d) The Supertonic Triad of A flat Major, in first inversion.

 e) The Dominant Triad of c sharp minor harmonic form, in second inversion.

 a)   b)   c)   d)   e)

5. Analyze this piece by answering the questions below.

Adagio e cantabile

Abigail's Waltz

S. McKibbon-U'Ren

Cadence: _____

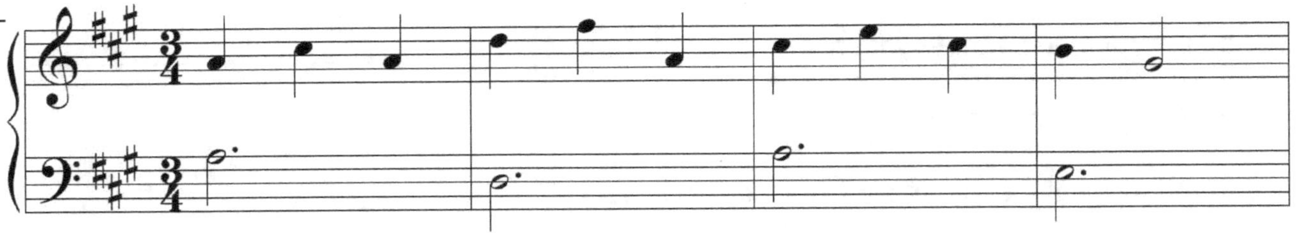

Cadence: _____

Cadence: _____

Cadence: _____

a) Label the two sections in this piece as A and B. Name the form: _____.

b) Mark the structural phrasing (4 four-measure phrases) in this piece.

c) Identify the type of each implied Cadence as Authentic or Half.

d) Explain the Tempo Mark. _____.

e) When performed, how many measures are played? _____.

1. For each line:

    a) Name the Key.
    ___
    10 b) Write the Root/Quality Chord Symbol above and the Functional Chord Symbol below.

Root/Quality
Chord Symbol: _____ _____ _____ _____ _____

Key: _____

Functional
Chord Symbol: _____ _____ _____ _____ _____

Root/Quality
Chord Symbol: _____ _____ _____ _____ _____

Key: _____

Functional
Chord Symbol: _____ _____ _____ _____ _____

2. Identify the Root, Quality (Major, minor or Dominant 7th) and Position of each Chord or Triad.

10

Root: _____ _____ _____ _____ _____

Quality: _____ _____ _____ _____ _____

Position: _____ _____ _____ _____ _____

Ultimate Music Theory
LEVEL 6 Supplemental Exam #8

3.   For the following Melodic Opening:

   a) Name the key of the melody.
   b) Write the Time Signature directly on the music.
10 c) Complete the first phrase. End on an unstable scale degree. (There will be more than one correct answer.)
   d) Compose an Answer Phrase to create a Parallel period. End on a stable scale degree. (There will be more than one correct answer.)
   e) Draw a phrase mark (slur) over each phrase.

Key: _____

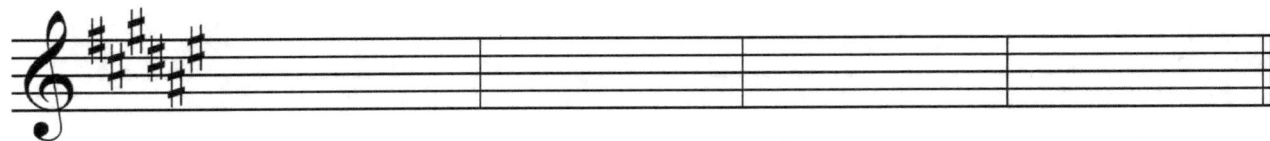

4.   For each of the following Melodic Phrases:

   a) Name the key of the melody.
   b) Write the Time Signature directly on the music.
10 c) Write the Root/Quality Chord Symbols implied by the melody on the lines above the music.
   d) Name the type of cadence (Authentic or Half) implied by the melody.

5. Analyze this excerpt from the Georg Philipp Telemann's Aria in G Major by answering the questions below.

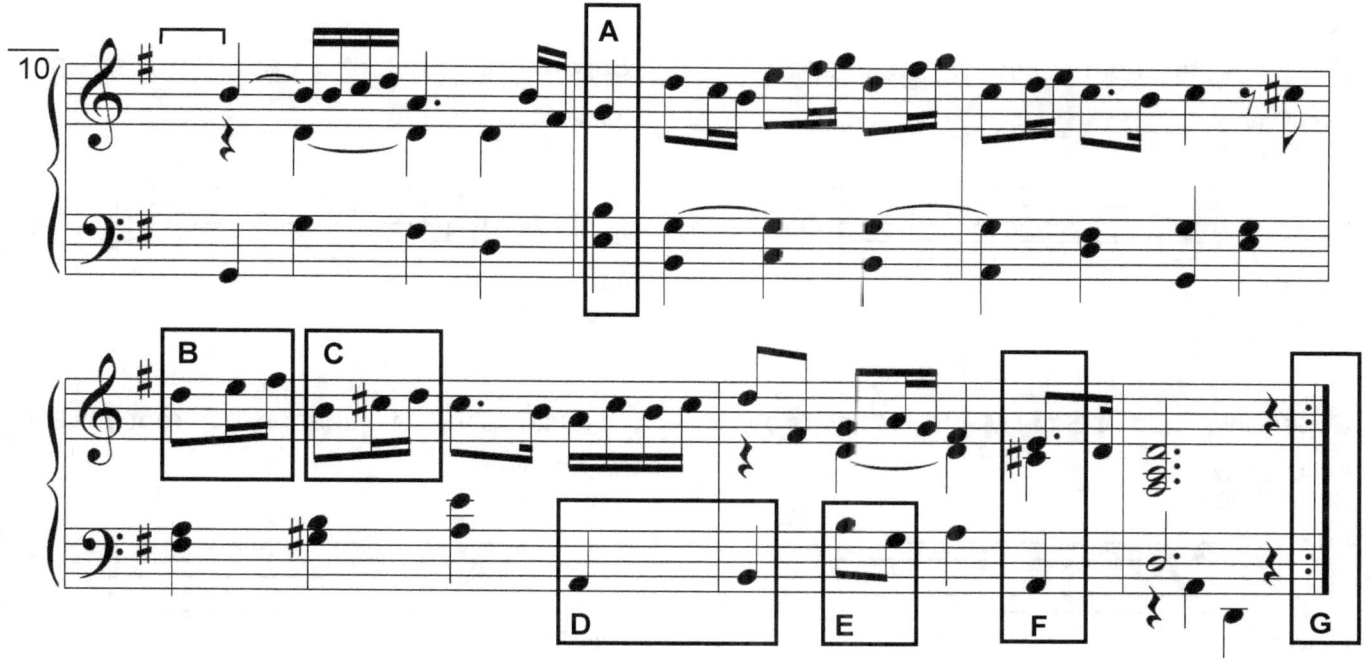

a) This excerpt is in Common Time. Write the Time Signature directly on the music.

b) Circle the correct Texture for this excerpt: Homophonic   or   Monophonic.

c) For the Triad at **A**, identify: Root: _____   Quality: _____   Position: _____ .

d) Circle the relationship of the melodic pattern at **B** and **C** as: Transposition   or   Inversion.

e) Identify the interval at **D**: _____.   Identify the interval at **E**: _____ .

f) For the Triad at **F**, identify: Root: _____   Quality: _____   Position: _____ .

g) Explain the sign at **G**: _____ .

h) Circle a Chromatic Half Step (Chromatic Semitone) directly on the music. Label it as CH.

i) Identify the number of: Ties: _____;   Quarter Rests: _____;   Eighth Rests: _____ .

j) How many times does the rhythmic pattern ♩ ♪ ♪ ♩ appear in this excerpt? _____ .

1. a) Write the following Solid (Blocked) Triads or Chords. Use a Key Signature and any necessary accidentals. Use whole notes. Write the Root/Quality Chord Symbol above and the Functional Chord Symbol below.

___
10

Dominant 7th Chord of f minor, root position.

Root/Quality
Chord Symbol: _____

Functional
Chord Symbol: _____

Subdominant Triad of D Major, 2nd inversion.

Root/Quality
Chord Symbol: _____

Functional
Chord Symbol: _____

Supertonic Triad of G flat Major, 1st inversion.

Root/Quality
Chord Symbol: _____

Functional
Chord Symbol: _____

Dominant Triad of d sharp minor, root position.

Root/Quality
Chord Symbol: _____

Functional
Chord Symbol: _____

Submediant Triad of f sharp minor, 2nd inversion.

Root/Quality
Chord Symbol: _____

Functional
Chord Symbol: _____

Subdominant Triad of b minor, 1st inversion.

Root/Quality
Chord Symbol: _____

Functional
Chord Symbol: _____

b) For each of the following Dominant Seventh Chords, name the Key. Write the Root/Quality Chord Symbol above and the Functional Chord Symbol below.

Root/Quality
Chord Symbol: _____   _____   _____   _____

Key: _____   _____   _____   _____

Functional
Chord Symbol: _____   _____   _____   _____

2. For each of the following Cadences:
    a) Name the key.
    b) Name the type of cadence (authentic or half).

Key: _____   _____   _____

Cadence: _____   _____   _____

3. a) Write the note that is a Chromatic Half Step (Chromatic Semitone) above each note.

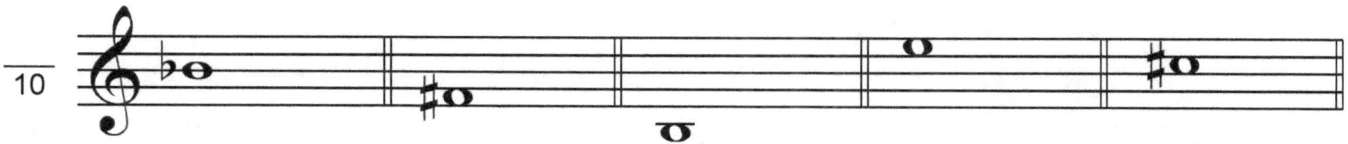

   b) Write the note that is a Diatonic Half Step (Diatonic Semitone) below each note.

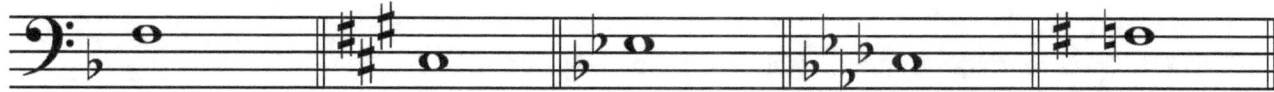

   c) Write the note that is a Whole Step (Whole Tone) below each note.

   d) Write the Enharmonic Equivalent for each note.

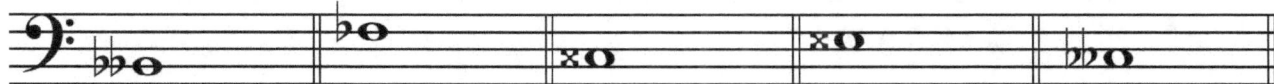

Ultimate Music Theory
LEVEL 6 Supplemental Bonus Exam

4.   Name the scale. Write the scale, ascending and descending, using the correct Key Signature and any necessary accidentals for each. Use whole notes.

___
10   a)   The Enharmonic Tonic Major scale of C Sharp Major is: _____.

b)   The Enharmonic Tonic Major scale of G flat Major is: _____.

c)   The minor scale, natural form, with E as the Subtonic is: _____.

d)   The Parallel minor scale, melodic form, of G Major is: _____.

e)   The Parallel Major scale of e flat minor is: _____.

Ultimate Music Theory
LEVEL 6 Supplemental Bonus Exam

5. a) Add rests below the brackets to complete each of the following measures.

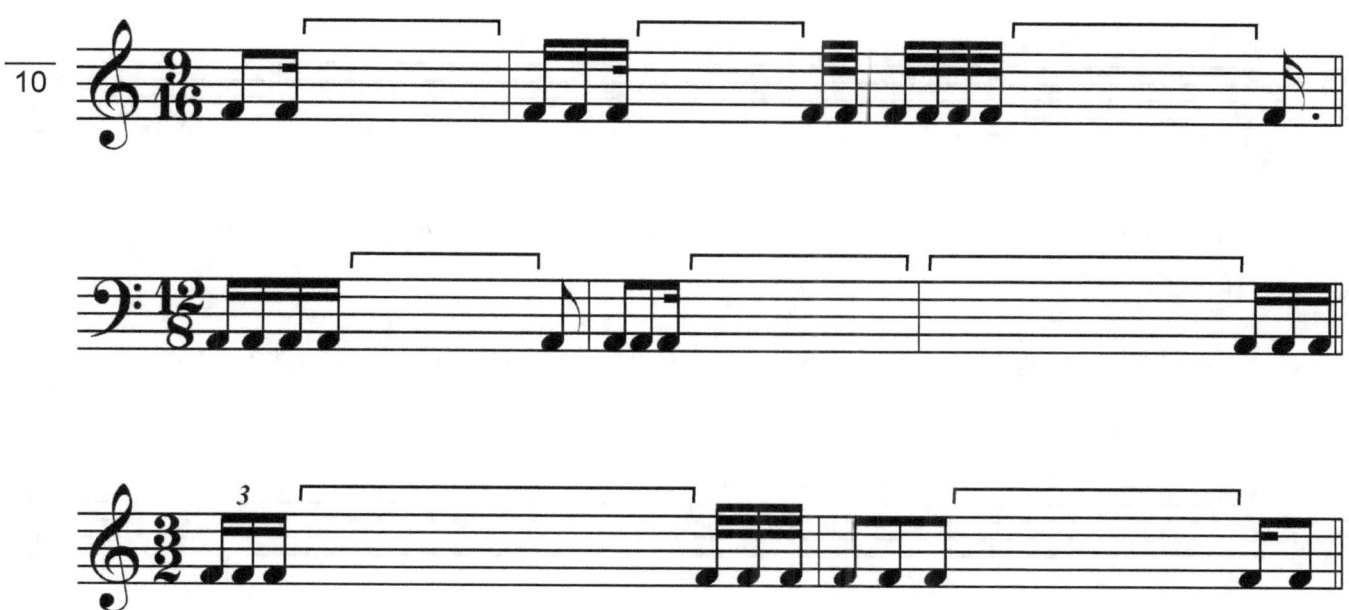

b) Add the correct Time Signature below each bracket to complete the following rhythms.

c) Add bar lines to complete the following rhythms.

6. a) Write the following Harmonic Intervals above each of the given notes. Use whole notes.

minor 3   Augmented 2   Perfect 1   Major 7   diminished 8

b) Write the following Melodic Intervals above each of the given notes. Use half notes.

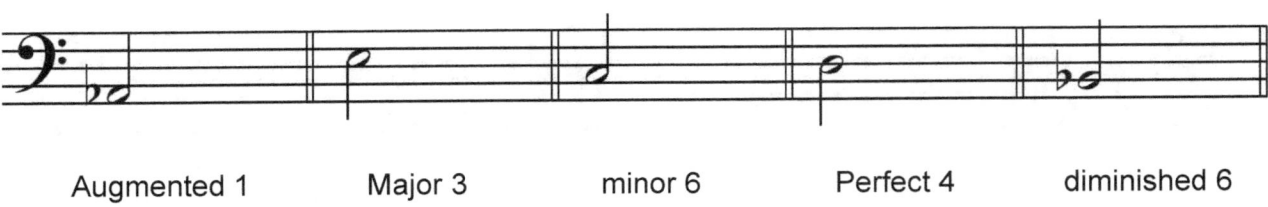

Augmented 1   Major 3   minor 6   Perfect 4   diminished 6

c) Name the following Harmonic Intervals.

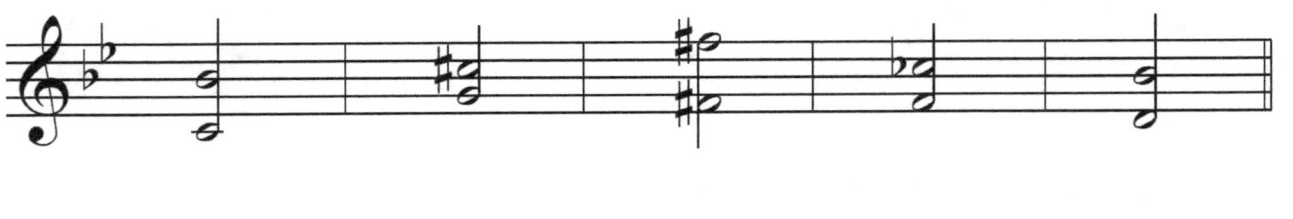

_____ _____ _____ _____ _____

d) Name the following Melodic Intervals.

_____ _____ _____ _____ _____

7. a) Name the Key of the following melody. Transpose the melody up a diminished third using the correct Key Signature. Name the new Key.

10

Key: _____

Key: _____

b) Name the Key of the following melody. Transpose it up into the Key of A flat Major using the correct Key Signature. Name the Interval of Transposition.

Key: _____

Interval of Transposition: _____

Ultimate Music Theory
LEVEL 6 Supplemental Bonus Exam

8. a) For the following Melodic Opening:
    i)   Name the key of this melody.
    ii) Complete the first phrase according to the given Functional Chord Symbols. End on an unstable scale degree. (There will be more than one correct answer.)
    iii) Compose an Answer phrase to create a Parallel Period. End on a stable scale degree. (There will be more than one correct answer.)
    iv) Draw a phrase mark (slur) over each phrase.

‾10‾

Key: _____

b) For the following phrases:
    i) Name the Key.
    ii) Write the Root/Quality Chord Symbols implied by the melody on the lines provided.

Key: _____

Key: _____

9. a) Draw one note that is equal in value to each of the following groups of notes.

___
10

i) ♫♫ = _____   ii) ⌐3¬ ♩♩♩ = _____

iii) = _____   iv) = _____

v) = _____   vi) = _____

vii) 𝅝 𝅝 𝅝 = _____   viii) = _____

ix) 3 = _____   x) = _____

b) Choose the correct description to conclude any FIVE (5) of the following statements:

i) Polyphonic Texture, Imitation, Sequences and Inversions are featured in:
☐ - Eine kleine Nachtmusic.   ☐ - Invention in C major, BWV 772.

ii) Ritornello Form, fast Scales, sweeping Arpeggios and a Cadenza are featured in:
☐ - Invention in C major, BWV 772.   ☐ - Brandenburg Concerto No. 5, 1st Movement.

iii) Homophonic Texture and Sonata Form are featured in:
☐ - Eine kleine Nachtmusic.   ☐ - Brandenburg Concerto No. 5, 1st Movement.

iv) Brandenburg Concerto No. 5, First Movement, was composed by:
☐ - W.A. Mozart.   ☐ - J.S. Bach.

v) Eine kleine Nachtmusik, K 525, First Movement, was composed by:
☐ - W.A. Mozart.   ☐ - J.S. Bach.

vi) Johann Sebastian Bach is a Composer from the:
☐ - Baroque Era.   ☐ - Classical Era.

vii) Wolfgang Amadeus Mozart is a Composer from the:
☐ - Baroque Era.   ☐ - Classical Era.

10. Analyze the following excerpt by answering the questions below.

Polonaise in G Minor

C. P. E. Bach

Allegro Moderato

___
10

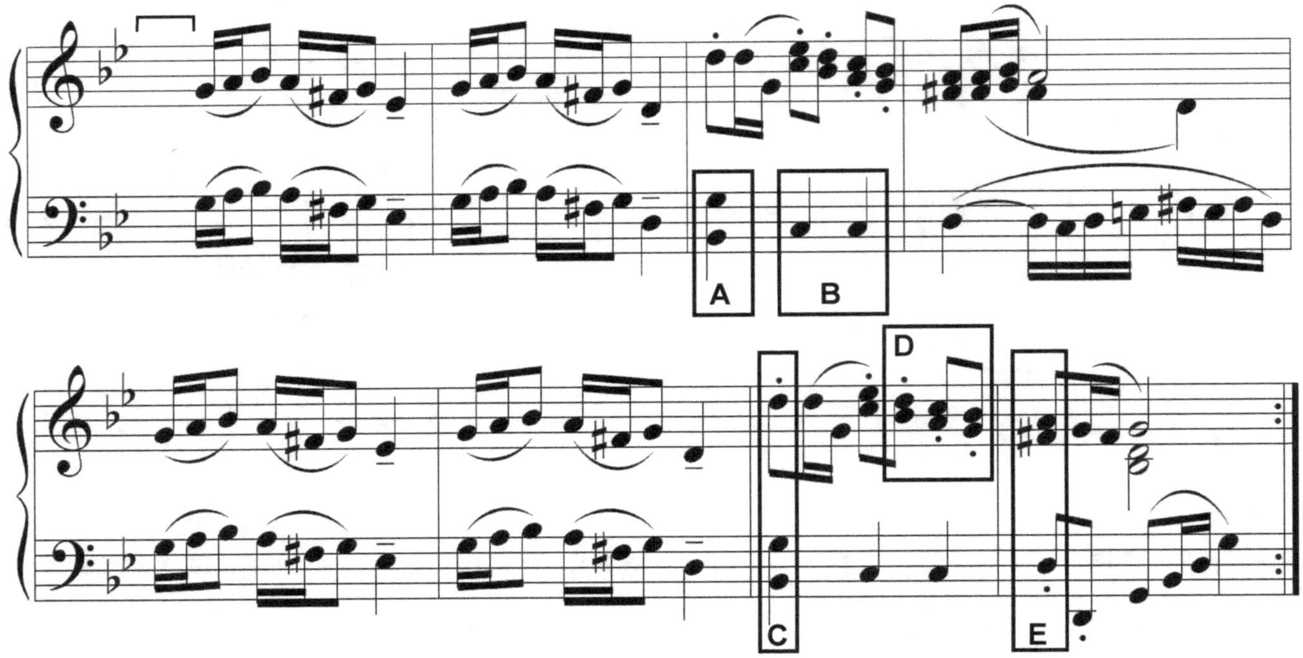

a) Write the Time Signature directly on the music.

b) Explain the Tempo Mark. _____.

c) Identify the motion between the RH and LH in Measure 1 as: Contrary   or   Parallel.

d) Identify the interval at letter **A**. _____.   Identify the interval at letter **B**. _____.

e) For the Triad at **C**, identify: Root: _____   Quality: _____   Position: _____.

f) Circle if the intervals at **D** are: Parallel 3rds   or   Parallel 6ths   or   Parallel 8ths.

g) For the Triad at **E**, identify: Root: _____   Quality: _____   Position: _____.

h) Circle if the relationship between mm. 1 - 4 and mm. 5 - 8 is: a and a1   or   a and b.

i) Circle a Diatonic Half Step (Diatonic Semitone) directly on the music. Label it as DH.

j) For this excerpt, identify the: Number of slurs (phrases): _____   Number of ties: _____.

TOP 10 Ultimate Music Theory Tips
To Score 100% on Exams

Tip #1: Students should complete at least 8 Practice Examinations before writing their Final Exam. LEVEL 6 Exams will have two hours to be completed.

Tip #2: Hold a "Practice Examination" in your studio. Have all students who are writing their Exams come at the same time. They can only bring a ruler, eraser and pencil. Set a Timer. When the timer starts, the examination begins – no talking, no cell phones, no open books!

Tip #3: Pizza Party! On the night before their Examinations, have a "Pizza Party" – Use the Ultimate Music Theory Flashcards App, UMT Whiteboard and UMT Games to review terminology and concepts. Everyone will have fun and everything will be fresh in their minds.

Tip #4: On Exam day, Students should arrive 15 minutes before the start time of their Examination.

Tip #5: If the Student is not given a piece of blank paper to use to write out their UMT Map before beginning their Examination, they should ask for one from the Exam Center Representative. (Have your Student practice asking for a blank piece of paper.)

Tip #6: Remind both Student and Parent that it is the Student's responsibility to bring a mechanical pencil (with extra lead), or 2 - 3 pencils (with a pencil sharpener), eraser and ruler. They cannot bring any items that have "music" on them, so they cannot bring their UMT Rulers.

Tip #7: It is always a good idea to bring a tissue or two, a bottle of water and a couple of hard candies if it is cold/allergy time. Be sure to get plenty of rest the day before the exam.

Tip #8: Complete the exam in order beginning with question 1. Review what your Student can do if they get stuck – if their brain goes blank on a question. One suggestion would be to continue to the next question and then go back later to finish that question.

Tip #9: Remind Students to look at the front AND back of each page to ensure that ALL questions have been answered... and checked... and double checked.

Tip #10: Ultimate Music Theory 100% Club - *The Way to Score Success!* You and your student can become a member of the UMT 100% Club when your student receives a score of 100% on their nationally recognized theory exams including the RCM Theory Examinations.

Go to UltimateMusicTheory.com and complete the UMT 100% Club Form
to receive your special 100% Club Certificate & Congratulations!

Workbooks, Exams, Answers, Online Courses, App & More!

A Proven Step-by-Step System to Learn Theory Faster - from Beginner to Advanced.

Innovative techniques designed to develop a complete understanding of music theory, to enhance sight reading, ear training, creativity, composition and musical expression.

All UMT Series have matching Answer Books!

The UMT Rudiments Series - Beginner A, Beginner B, Beginner C, Prep 1, Prep 2, Basic, Intermediate, Advanced & Complete (All-In-One)

♪ 12 Lessons, Review Tests, and a Final Exam to develop confidence
♪ Music Theory Guide & Chart for fast and easy reference of theory concepts
♪ 80 Flashcards for fun drills to dramatically increase retention & comprehension

Rudiments Exam Series - Preparatory, Basic, Intermediate & Advanced

♪ 8 Exams plus UMT Tips on How to Score 100% on Theory Exams

Each Rudiments Workbook correlates to a Supplemental Workbook.

The UMT Supplemental Series - Prep Level, Level 1, Level 2, Level 3, Level 4, Level 5, Level 6, Level 7, Level 8 & Complete (All-In-One) Level

♪ Form & Analysis and Music History - Composers, Eras & Musical Styles
♪ Melody Writing using ICE - Imagine, Compose & Explore
♪ 12 Lessons, Review Tests, Final Exam and 80 Flashcards for quick study

Supplemental Exam Series - Level 5, Level 6, Level 7 & Level 8

♪ 8 Exams to successfully prepare for nationally recognized Theory Exams

UMT Online Courses, Music Theory App & More

♪ UMT Certification Course, Teachers Membership & Elite Educator Program
♪ Ultimate Music Theory App correlates to the Rudiments Workbooks
♪ Free Resources - Teachers Guide, Music Theory Blogs, videos & downloads

Go To: UltimateMusicTheory.com